A ROOKIE READER ®

BEARS, BEARS, EVERYWHERE

By Rita Milios

Illustrations by Tom Dunnington

Prepared under the direction of Robert Hillerich, Ph.D.

 CHILDRENS PRESS ®

CHICAGO

LIBRARY OF CONGRESS
Library of Congress Cataloging-in-Publication Data
Milios, Rita.
    Bears, bears, everywhere / by Rita Milios ; illustrated by Tom Dunnington.
        p. cm. — (A Rookie Reader)
    Summary: An observer of one bear in the air, two bears on the stairs, counts all the way up to ten bears huffing and puffing and is relieved that they're full of stuffing.
    ISBN 0-516-02085-4 (lib. bdg.)   0-516-42085-2 (pbk.)
    [1. Teddy bears—Fiction. 2. Counting. 3. Stories in rhyme.] I. Dunnington, Tom, ill. II Title. III. Series.
PZ8.3.M59Be   1988
[E]—dc19   87-33780
                                      CIP
                                      AC

16 17 18 19 20 R 03 02 01

One bear in the air.

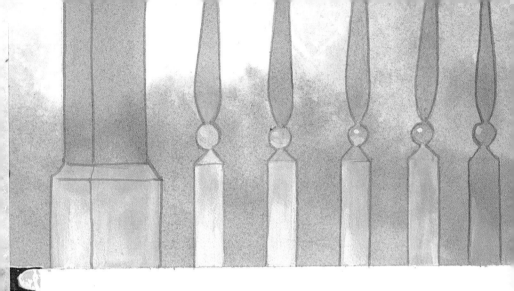

Two bears on the stairs.

Look! I see three in a tree.

8

There are four more
behind the door.

Five bears in a chair.

Bears, bears, everywhere.

Six bears wearing pajamas.

Seven bears crying for their mamas.

Eight bears hungry as can be.

Nine bears running after me.

Bears here. Bears there.

23

Bears, bears, everywhere.

Ten bears huffing and puffing.

I'm so glad they're full of stuffing!

WORD LIST

a	eight	look	six
after	everywhere	mamas	so
air	five	me	stairs
and	for	more	stuffing
are	four	nine	ten
as	full	of	the
be	glad	on	their
bear(s)	here	one	there
behind	huffing	pajamas	they're
can	hungry	puffing	three
chair	I	running	tree
crying	I'm	see	two
door	in	seven	wearing

About the Author

Rita Milios lives in Toledo, Ohio with her husband and two grade-school children. She is a free-lance writer and instructor in the Continuing Education department at Toledo University. She has published numerous articles in magazines including *McCall's, Lady's Circle,* and *The Writer.* She is currently working on her first adult book. Mrs. Milios is the author of *Sleeping and Dreaming* in the New True Book series and *I Am* and *Bears, Bears Everywhere* in the Rookie Reader series.

About the Artist

Tom Dunnington hails from the Midwest, having lived in Minnesota, Iowa, Illinois, and Indiana. He attended the John Herron Institute of Art in Indianapolis and the American Academy of Art and the Chicago Art Institute in Chicago. He has been an art instructor and illustrator for many years. In addition to illustrating books, Mr. Dunnington is working on a series of paintings of endangered birds (produced as limited edition prints). His current residence is in Oak Park, Illinois, where he works as a free-lance illustrator and is active in church and community youth work.